S RULES

For Kids

Author Tony R. Smith

SOCCER
REFEREE SIGNALS

Referee

SOCCER REFEREE SIGNALS

Indirect
Free Kick

SOCCER REFEREE SIGNALS

Direct
Free Kick

SOCCER REFEREE SIGNALS

Yellow
Card

SOCCER REFEREE SIGNALS

Red
Card

SOCCER REFEREE SIGNALS

Play On

SOCCER REFEREE SIGNALS

Penalty Kick

SOCCER
REFEREE SIGNALS

Offside

SOCCER REFEREE SIGNALS

Offside Location

SOCCER REFEREE SIGNALS

Substitution

SOCCER
REFEREE SIGNALS

Goal

SOCCER REFEREE SIGNALS

Disallowed
Goal

SOCCER REFEREE SIGNALS

Time-out

Corner Kick

SOCCER REFEREE SIGNALS

Jumping

SOCCER REFEREE SIGNALS

Obstruction

SOCCER REFEREE SIGNALS

Pushing

SOCCER REFEREE SIGNALS

Hand Ball

SOCCER
REFEREE SIGNALS

Tripping

SOCCER REFEREE SIGNALS

Kicking

SCOOCER SKILLS

BASIC BALL HANDLING SKILLS

BALL HANDLING SKILLS

MORE BALL HANDLING SKILLS

KICK AND
SCORE MOVE

DEFENSE TO
STOP SCORE

Set up for
defense

TIME TO
SCORE

DRIBBLING
ON THE MOVE

KICK AND
SCORE

DRIBBLING
DOWN FIELD

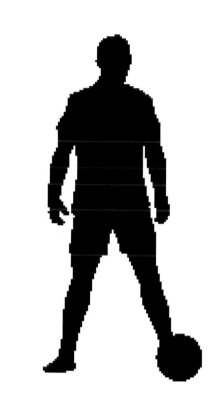

WAITING TO SET UP

DRIBBLING
UP THE FIELD

BONUS NOTEBOOK

PLAYER OR COACH NOTES

PLAYER OR COACH NOTES

PLAYER OR COACH NOTES

PLAYER OR COACH NOTES

PLAYER OR COACH NOTES

PLAYER OR COACH NOTES

PLAYER OR COACH NOTES

PLAYER OR COACH NOTES

PLAYER OR COACH NOTES

PLAYER OR COACH NOTES

PLAYER OR COACH NOTES

BONUS PRACTICE TIMES

WORKOUT/PRACTICE TIMES

WORKOUT/PRACTICE TIMES

_____

_____

_____

_____

_____

_____

_____

_____

_____

_____

_____

_____

_____

_____

WORKOUT/PRACTICE TIMES

_____   _____

_____   _____

_____   _____

_____   _____

_____   _____

_____   _____

_____   _____

_____   _____

_____   _____

_____   _____

_____   _____

_____   _____

_____   _____

_____   _____

_____   _____

WORKOUT/PRACTICE TIMES

WORKOUT/PRACTICE TIMES

WORKOUT/PRACTICE TIMES

WORKOUT/PRACTICE TIMES

_____

_____

_____

_____

_____

_____

_____

_____

_____

_____

_____

_____

_____

_____

_____

_____

_____

_____

_____

_____

_____

_____

_____

_____

WORKOUT/PRACTICE TIMES

_____   _____

_____   _____

_____   _____

_____   _____

_____   _____

_____   _____

_____   _____

_____   _____

_____   _____

_____   _____

_____   _____

_____   _____

_____   _____

_____   _____

_____   _____

WORKOUT/PRACTICE TIMES

WORKOUT/PRACTICE TIMES

WORKOUT/PRACTICE TIMES

_____   _____

_____   _____

_____   _____

_____   _____

_____   _____

_____   _____

_____   _____

_____   _____

_____   _____

_____   _____

_____   _____

_____   _____

_____   _____

_____   _____

WORKOUT/PRACTICE TIMES

WORKOUT/PRACTICE TIMES

_____   _____

_____   _____

_____   _____

_____   _____

_____   _____

_____   _____

_____   _____

_____   _____

_____   _____

_____   _____

_____   _____

_____   _____

_____   _____

_____   _____

Made in United States
North Haven, CT
26 August 2022

23282322R00035